I0420212

Muslim Agents of Statecrafting a Civilization

Nassef Manabilang Adiong

Co-IRIS (International Relations and Islamic Studies Research Cohort)

Abstract: This article focuses on the salient agent (Virtuous Ruler/Shah/Supreme Leader/King) basing from the works of Al-Farabi (The Perfect State), Ferdowsi (The Epic of Kings), Al-Mawardi (The Ordinances of Government), and Nizam al-Mulk (The Book of Government or Rules for Kings). The study will first delineate their perspectives about the subject-matter (i.e. the institutional elites in statecraft), and then the author will compare and contrast their views including his own analysis as well. Selected comparative sections that pertain to the traceable criteria and processes of their views in order to complement an able and effective agent of statecrafting a civilization are presented.

Key words: nation-state, head of state, Islamicate civilization, political elites, government

INTRODUCTION

Civilization may be regarded as a composition of multiple nation-states [1] converged by homogeneous factors of belief system, religion, culture, and development in science and technology. The progress may originate from the evolution and utilization of language (oral v. written literatures), literary and intellectual histories of thinkers/authors and of their unique local knowledge, and the geo-political and human conditions of a particular age that lead to the axial transition of a certain civilization. The origins of progress caused the emergence of axial transition or moment in every civilization is introduced by Robert N. Bellah [2]. Moreover, the sustainability of life (temporal period) of a civilization lies to the skillful art of effective statecrafting by established institutions.

Statecraft is the skillful ability by institutions to manage both domestic and international affairs of the state. An institution can be tripartite democracy (i.e., having equal executive, legislative, and judicial representations), theocracy (a religious organization is considered the head of the state), nomocracy (i.e., the government is based on the authority or rule of law within society), or monarchy (the rulers are elite families considered of having royal blood). The optimal agents of statecrafting influence institutions of polity and economy including governmental regularities and behaviors of societies and of communities under their own territorial jurisdiction.

According to Shmuel N. Eisenstadt [3], the central analytical core of the term civilization - as distinct from such social formations as political regimes, different forms of political economy or collectivities like 'tribes,' ethnic groups or nations, and from religion or cultural traditions - is the combination of ontological or cosmological visions, of visions of trans-mundane and mundane reality, with the definition, construction, and regulation of the major arenas of social life and interaction. However, Marshall G.S. Hodgson [4] contended that civilization is "a relatively extensive grouping of interrelated cultures, insofar as they have shared in cumulative traditions in the form of high culture on the urban, literate level; a culture, that is, such as that of historical India or Europe taken as cultural wholes. Such groups of peoples have varied greatly among themselves and yet have shared broadly cultural and historical experiences differing decisively from those of more distant peoples."

And the sustenance of high culture can be glued through a form of solidarity or sense of belongingness which was studied and extrapolated by Ibn Khaldun [5] through his notion of *asabiyah*. This term refers to social solidarity with an emphasis on amalgamation, collective consciousness and sense of shared purpose and values, and social cohesion, originally in a context of tribal culture, clans, and/or clientship (mutual patronage to the whole community). [6] Norbert Elias [7] contended that one of the elements of civilizing process is state formation. This element looks into the causes of increasingly centralized nations which also includes interconnected web of societies that comprises the process of statecraft. The succeeding essays will tackle the perspectives of Al-Farabi, Ferdowsi, Al-Mawardi, and Nizam al-Mulk regarding their agent (virtuous ruler/shah/supreme leader/king) of statecrafting a civilization. After the presentation of their essays, the last essay analyzes the comparisons about their views on leadership by comparing sections on selection, qualification, and responsibility which are commonly represented in their works; while a section on other observations are those of unique or distinct to a particular author's work such as al-

Farabi's settings of virtuous and imperfect states and Nizam al-Mulk's boon-companions and their roles concomitant to the king.

The Virtuous Ruler of Al-Farabi: Al-Farabi's perfect leader is a virtuous ruler that has the combined characteristics of theoretical capability or inclination of a philosopher (i.e. to educate the elites) and charismatic or persuasive power of a prophet (i.e. to influence the masses). Most of his works on political philosophy were his preferred criteria on selecting a virtuous ruler. And this can be reviewed in one of his books on political philosophy, which is: Al-Farabi [8]. *The Perfect State: Mabadi' ara' ahl al-Madina al-Faḍila: A Revised Text with Introduction, Translation, and Commentary.* Trans. Richard Walzer. Gloucestershire, UK: Clarendon Press, 1985.

In the fields of ethics and politics, a number of treatises were written by him. The list opens with the Opinions of the Inhabitants of the Virtuous State (*Ara' Ahl al-Madınah al-Fadilah*) and the Civil Polity (*al-Siyasah al-Madaniyah*), and includes an Epitome of Plato's Laws (*Kitab al-Nawamıs*), select sections on politics (*Fusul Murtaza'ah min Aqawıl al-Qudama'*), a treatise on the Attainment of Happiness (*Tahsıl al-Sa'adah*) and a shorter tract entitled

5

Admonition to Seek the Path of Happiness (*al-Tanbıh 'ala Sabıl al-Sa'adah*). [9]

He is popularly known as "the second teacher," while Aristotle was the first. Moreover, al-Farabi commented on many of Aristotle's works and wrote a number of independent works. [10] He grew up during the reign of Nasr I ibn Ahmad of the Samanid dynasty which considered itself as Persian, and has been associated in Islamic history with learning. In Bukhara, he pursued his advanced study of fiqh, music, and later religious sciences. Upon completing his studies, he became a qadi (judge), but he abandoned his job and left for Baghdad in his early forties to study philosophy and logic.

Robert Hammond [11] added that the political philosophy of Al-Farabi is a mixture of Platonic and Aristotelian elements. The main Platonic element in al-Farabi's political theory is to put all humanity in one universal state, which is an organized humanity without national boundaries and not ruled by a particular king but by God.

Selection: Al-Farabi premised his political treatise stating that humans cannot attain perfection because they are destined to go outside the framework of political association [12] or in al-Farabi's

[13] words "societies of people." Human's very nature is not to live alone but the need of constant help from other humans to provide him/her needs. This brings them together in a community where everybody needs each other to survive and attain perfection. His idea on political association is directed towards attainment of true happiness such as pleasure and acquisition of wealth. In other words, a virtuous ruler is selected out of necessity in a community, especially if he displays intellectual capacity of a philosopher and charisma of a prophet.

Consequently, leadership for al-Farabi entails that not all citizens (part of the society) are capable of becoming leaders of the state; only the most perfect person in the community or one who has the most number of good qualities can hold the position of being the leader. He also preferred a head of state to exist first and then to have people for him to lead.

Qualification: According to al-Farabi, the ruler is the source of all power and knowledge. Al-Farabi writes:

> *"... the virtuous ruler without qualification is he who does not need anyone to rule him in anything whatever, but has*

actually acquired the sciences and every kind of knowledge, and has no need of man to guide him in anything. He is able to comprehend well each one of the particular things that he ought to do. He is able to guide well all others to everything in which he instructs them, to employ all those who do any of the acts for which they are equipped, and to determine, define, and direct these acts toward happiness." [14]

Moreover, he stated that no one can be a ruler if he lacks the power of imagination of which the prophet is the most accomplished representative. The philosopher who lacks it is a false philosopher because the absence of this faculty forms a serious defect that leaves him incapable of governing the state and educating the masses. Hence, the philosophic and prophetic faculties constitute, for al-Farabi, the first and necessary requirement that the virtuous ruler must fulfill. In the Virtuous State, however, al-Farabi enumerates twelve other qualities the virtuous ruler must acquire. These, in brief, are as follows. [15]

1. Perfect and sound bodily organs that can perform their function with ease.

2. Sound understanding that enables him to grasp the intention of the speaker.

3. Good memory that retains what he understands, sees, hears and perceives.

4. Intelligence and keenness of mind which allows him to grasp the reality of a certain situation with the minimum of indicative signs.

5. Eloquence which assists him in articulating his thoughts.

6. Love of education so that he is not burdened by the effort accompanying learning.

7. Moderation in matters of food, drink and sex, as well as natural shunning of levity and of pleasures caused by these things.

8. Love of truth and truthful people and dislike of lying and liars.

9. Natural magnanimity and repugnance of meanness.

10. Indifference to money and all other worldly pleasures.

11. Natural love of justice and just people and abhorrence of injustice and unjust people; to treat other people like he treats his family, that is, without any discrimination and

to see justice is done to oppressed whoever he is; being easy to bend but difficult to bend to oppression or evil.

12. Possession of firm resolution and the courage to do what he believes must be done.

In addition to these twelve innate attributes, al-Farabi enumerates in the aphorisms six other "conditions" that must be possessed by the ruler. These conditions, unlike the attributes, do not emerge until after maturity. They are: wisdom, perfect practical wisdom, excellence of the faculty of persuasion, excellence of producing a representative imagination of the truth, power to fight holy war in person, and the absence of any physical impediments which would prevent him from attending matters about holy war.[16]

Responsibility: The virtuous ruler must assign positions to the various inhabitants, each according to his merit, either in a subservient or in a ruling position. The task of the virtuous ruler is to strive to eliminate evil from the state because happiness is "the good qualification" for the disappearance of all evil, whether natural or voluntary. In his attempt to destroy voluntary evil and to bring the good into existence, the virtuous ruler employs two methods: instruction and the formation of character. [17]

By instruction, al-Farabi means the introduction of theoretical virtues in the state. For without education, no citizen can attain perfection and happiness. The second method is the formation of the character of the citizens. It is the means by which moral virtues are introduced in the state. This involves habituating the citizens to do virtuous acts that become dispositions representing "the practical states of character." In order to habituate the citizens to what is right; the virtuous ruler must employ persuasive arguments that help establish these acts and states of character in the soul completely so as to arouse the resolution to do acts willingly.

What al-Farabi is saying is that, in order for the virtuous ruler to instruct the elite and form their character, he ought to be a philosopher skilled in the speculative sciences, and in order for him to instruct the masses and form their character, he ought to be a prophet who possesses persuasion and imagination to perfection.

Virtuous and Imperfect States: A virtuous state is compared by Al-Farabi to a perfect and healthy body whose organs differed in their natural functions. The heart is the master organ and is in the first rank, while the lower organs are in the second rank functioning with the aim of perfecting the first rank; and the lower organs being served by much lower organs performing their functions for the perfection of the second rank. It is similar to a state where a human master is being served by his subordinates, and the former in turn is being served by the lowest category of subordinates who are not being served by anybody. [18]

He also identified four imperfect states: The first is the ignorant state, which is one in which the inhabitants do not know what real happiness is and therefore cannot seek it, but are lured by false pleasures in life (e.g. personal safety or self-preservation, wealth, pleasure, honor, conquest, freedom or lawlessness); the second is ruined state, one in which the inhabitants know what is happiness but fail to live up to it and so they behave like those in the ignorant state. They know the good but they do contemptible things. The third is the declined state, which is one in which the inhabitants were originally living according to the concept of the perfect state but have regressed through time. And the last is the lost (misled) state, which is one in which the inhabitants have never achieved happiness and/or have no concept of God. They are ruled by a false leader who resorts to trickery and deception in attaining his goals.

The Shah of Ferdowsi: Epics serve as one of the tools in marking the axial moment of a nation or civilization. It connects someone's past to present via channels of oral or written literatures. Thus, it represents the heritage of people's collective memory which linked them to their past to present, and guides them to their future. According to Farhat-Holzman, [19] epics have always played the role of giving a people a sense of their historic continuity, a sense of language and its appropriate literary form, and above all, their earliest sense of peoplehood – which in some cases took the form of early nationalism. Some examples of notable epics are the Sumerian Gilgamesh, the Hebrew Bible's story of David and Goliath, the Aeneid, the Spanish epic of El Cid, the French Song of Roland, etc.

Hakim Abul-Qasim Firdausi Tusi or simply Ferdowsi wrote and collected Shahname, [20] which is indeed a classic of its own – with its own style and wonderful literary form. It provided foundational history, cultural heritage, and national identity all throughout the Persian world, i.e., from Iran, Central Asia, to Pakistan and India. In addition, it also reflects Persian values, its ancient religion, its sense of nationhood, and use of Persian language at the point in their history when they had lost their national independence from the onslaught of Arabic and Islam. [21]

The Shahname has 62 stories, 990 chapters, and contains 60,000 rhyming couplets, making it more than seven times the length of Homer's Iliad, and more than twelve times the length of the German Nibelungenlied. [22] It is structured according to the mythical and historical reign of 50 Persian Kings. The epic can be roughly divided into three parts: the first part tells of the mythical creation of Persia and its earliest mythical past; the second part tells of the legendary Kings and the heroes Rustem and Sohrab; the third part blends historical fact with legend, telling of the semi-mythical adventures of actual historical Kings. [23]

Ferdowsi used pre-Islamic sources for his epic in an Islamic Iran. He wrote his poem in Persian rather than Arabic, creating a national epic that reconstructed the history and myth of the ancient Persian peoples. Consequently, the Shahname has an important place in Persian culture and in the hearts of Persian people. One of the functions of the "Epic of the Kings" is to protect and preserve the

Persian collective memory, language, and culture in a turbulent sea of many historical storms and challenges of modern times, e.g., globalization. For over a thousand years Persians, Afghanis, Azeris, Georgians, Tajiks, Kurds, and a myriad of other ethnic groups have continued to read and listen to recitations from Shahnameh.

Selection: In this epic of kings, a shah can be selected either by the incumbent shah or through familial hereditary process. The first chapter (the Shahs of Old) until the last chapter (the Death of Rustem) indicated that the first shah emerged with Kaiumers when he first sat upon the throne of Persia and automatically became the master of the world. [24] Then, Husheng [25] was selected by Kaiumers to lead his army against Deev [26] who killed his son, Saiamuk. After Husheng left the world, Jemshid [27] became the shah and ruled the world for more than 700 years. He was automatically appointed because his father, Tahumers, was the previous shah. Feridoun and his sons, Zal, and Rustem are some of the notable shahs who ruled the world (Persia). Below is an excerpt on how Jemshid immediately became the shah:

"Howbeit when Tahumers had sat upon the golden throne for the space of thirty years he passed away, but his works endured; and Jemshid, his glorious son, whose heart was filled with the counsels of his father, came after him. Now Jemshid reigned over the land seven hundred years girt with might, and Deevs, birds, and Peris obeyed him." [28]

Qualification: There are two recurring characteristics in Ferdowsi's collection for an individual to qualify for the position of shah: intelligence (i.e. having the necessary knowledge for an effective public administration and care for the welfare of his fellow subjects) and courage (i.e. salient bravery to protect his subjects, manifest strong will and determination, and potentiality in standing against threats, enemies, and misconceptions). For example, Husheng is the intelligent shah who ruled Persia for 40 years as explained in this excerpt:

"Now Husheng was a wise man and just, and the heavens revolved over his throne forty years. Justice did he spread over the land, and the world was better for his reign. For he first gave to men fire, and showed them how to draw it from

out the stone; and he taught them how they might lead the rivers, that they should water the land and make it fertile; and he bade them till and reap. And he divided the beasts and paired them and gave them names." [29]

The second one is courage as shown in the seven heroic trials [30] of Rustem [31].

1. *The lion:* Rakush [32] gallops two days travel in one day. They rest and a lion appears. Rakush kills the lion while Rustem sleeps. [33]

2. *The desert:* Rakush and Rustem got lost in a dry desert and nearly died of thirst. Their prayers brought a sheep who leads them to a stream. [34]

3. *The dragon:* While Rustem sleeps, a dragon appears. Rakush strikes his hoof on the ground, the dragon vanishes and Rustem awakes. Finally, Rustem sees the dragon. Rakush bites the dragon and Rustem cuts off its head. [35]

4. *The witch:* They find a banquet of food spread out under some trees and sit down to eat. A beautiful woman appears welcoming them. Rustem praises her beauty and God for

creating her. But she changes shape into a hideous terrifying hag. Rustem catches her and kills her.

5. *Battle with Ulad:* While Rustem sleeps Rakush wanders into a field and starts eating the crops. The farmer is furious. Rustem fights the farmer and pulls off his ears. The farmer gets the hero, Ulad, to represent him. Ulad arrives with a whole army. Rustem destroys the whole army single-handedly. He then asks Ulad if he knows where King Kavus is being held. Ulad is so impressed with Rustem he offers to be his guide and protector.

6. *Demon King Arzhang:* They come upon a demon encampment. Rustem and Rakush kill the demon king Arzhang and the other demons run away. They continue on the long journey to King Kavus.

7. *The White Demon:* King Kavus's castle is besieged by demons. Rustem waits until dawn comes and the demons fall asleep. He kills them. They capture the White Demon and cut out his liver. Kavus is set free. [36]

Responsibility: The primary duty of the shah is to protect his kingdom from insecurities such as poverty, famine, threats from external forces (impending invasions), and maintain stability, peace and order all over his territorial jurisdiction. This is more elaborated from the 700-year reign [37] of Jemshid [38].

He had command over all the angels and demons of the Persian world, and was both king and high priest. Excerpt: *"Now Jemshid reigned over the land seven hundred years girt with might, and Deevs, birds, and Peris obeyed him."* *[39]* He was responsible for several inventions that made life more secure for his people: the manufacture of armor and weapons, the weaving and dyeing of clothes of linen, silk and wool, the building of houses of brick, the mining of jewels and precious metals, the making of perfumes and wine, the navigation of the waters of the world in sailing ships. In short, humanity had risen to a great civilization in Jamshid's time.

Excerpt from the section of Jemshid's regime:

"And the world was happier for his sake, and he too was glad, and death was unknown among men, neither did they wot of pain or sorrow.... And the year also he divided into periods. And by aid of the Deevs he raised mighty works, and

Persepolis was builded by him, that to this day is called Tukht-e-Jemsheed, which being interpreted meaneth the throne of Jemshid. Then, when these things were accomplished, men flocked from all corners of the earth around his throne to do him homage and pour gifts before his face. And Jemshid prepared a feast, and bade them keep it, and calledit Neurouz, which is the New Day, and the people of Persia keep it to this hour. And Jemshid's power increased, and the world was at peace, and men beheld in him nought but what was good." [40]

In addition, Jemshid also divided the people into four groups: The priests, who conducted the worship of Hormozd; the warriors, who protected the people by the might of their arms; the farmers, who grew the grain that fed the people; and the artisans, who produced goods for the ease and enjoyment of the people. Excerpt: *"And he first parcelled out men into classes; priests, warriors, artificers, and husbandmen did he name them." [41]*

Punishment: The shah is reprimanded or punished if his heart and mind are full of hatred (i.e. perpetual vengeance against his enemies), greed of power and wealth, and unfaithful to God. As it is shown in this excerpt, Jemshid was punished by God and replaced him with Ahriman.

> *"Then it came about that the heart of Jemshid was uplifted in pride, and he forgot whence came his weal and the source of his blessings. He beheld only himself upon the earth, and he named himself God, and sent forth his image to be worshipped. But when he had spoken thus, the Mubids, which are astrologers and wise men, hung their heads in sorrow, and no man knew how he should answer the Shah. And God withdrew his hand from Jemshid, and the kings and the nobles rose up against him, and removed their warriors from his court, and Ahriman had power over the land."* [42]

The Supreme Leader of Al-Mawardi: Abu al-Hasan al-Mawardi was born on 364 AH/974 CE in Basra (located in present-day Iraq) and died on 450 AH/1058 CE in Baghdad located in the same country. [43] He grew up and served the Abbasid Caliphate and the

Buyids, and witnessed the zenith of the Fatimids and the rise of the Saljuqs. Literally, he experienced a polarized Ummah (an imagined unified community of believers of Islam) where political turmoil, conflicts, anomie, and social problems plagued the entire Muslim core regions from Arabia to North Africa.

However, this did not stop al-Mawardi's determination to become one of the highly respected scholar in Islamic jurisprudence. He enjoyed the respect and trust of Caliphs and Buyids alike, both of whom resorted to him for mediation, asked him to hold negotiations with their rivals, and took advantage of his diplomatic skills as ambassador. [44] He served as judge in several Iraqi districts and was awarded the honorary title of "Judge par excellence (*aqda al-quda*)" and was known as independent thinker (*mujtahid*) in religious matters.

The book is primarily al-Mawardi's attempt to interpret the existing political order through an Islamic framework, where the Caliphate is the ideal form of government that safeguard and implement the rules of shari'ah (or mostly Islamic legislation). Thus, it should upholds faith (derived from the revealed law) and manages the affairs of the world (derived from human law or reason and rationality). This was necessary in order to reassure people that, despite the apparent weakness of the Caliphs, the society in which they were living and the authorities to which they were submitting were legitimate in Islamic terms.

Since al-Mawardi believed that the authority of governors, judges and administrators was dependent on their appointment by a legitimate Caliph, the legitimacy of the caliphate must be preserved at all costs. Without this reassurance, people would lose faith in government institutions, including the courts, and might resort to civil unrest or schismatic religious sects, like the Fatimids. [45]

Selection: There are two ways [46] to determine the supreme leader (Imam or King): selection by the electors or appointment by a predecessor. The electors, a collective body, will select a supreme leader (king) for the nation. Members of the electors must demonstrate its probity (the quality of having strong moral principles, honesty, and decency), knowledge leading to recognition of the person fitted by his qualifications for the post of supreme leader, and prudence and wisdom likely to make them choose the best candidate and the most capable and knowledgeable in managing state affairs. [47]

With regards to the number [48] of electors, there are contestations among scholars, some argued for the "generality" in order for his election to be unanimously approved and his authority universally accepted, few argued for a minimum number of five as predicated by Abu Bakr and Umar's experiences, while scholars from Kufa argued for only three persons basing from a marriage contract, and others argued for a single person citing the experience of Ali.

Once the supreme leader is determined, if he accepts, the electors pledge their allegiance to him and his assumption of office takes effect immediately, but if he declines, other candidates are approached instead. If there is a tie in the result of the election, age (the older one is given precedence) and the quality (courage and knowledge) are the determining factors in selecting the sole winner. [49] Moreover, electors may not cast their votes if uncertainty persists following investigation that neither candidate can establish his temporal advantage because al-Mawardi believed that the office of supreme leader is a contract and that sovereignty may not be shared. [50]

With regards to appointment by the predecessor (or the validity of succession [51]), scholars have different opinions. [52] Some Iraqi jurists tend to directly accept the legitimacy of the successor even without the proper selection process of the electors. However, majority of jurists and theologians argued that the establishment in office could only take place as a result of 'free choice' by the electors because they believed that the office of the sovereign is an appointment that is conferred by someone empowered to do that. [53]

Qualification: Al-Mawardi imposed seven conditions [54] (as supported by Islamic traditions) of eligibility for supreme leadership: first, justice or probity with all its attributes; second, knowledge conducive to the exercise of independent judgment in crises or decision-making; third, sound hearing, vision and speech so that perception could serve as a correct basis for action; fourth, physical fitness and freedom from handicaps to movement or agility of action; fifth, prudence that ensures wise handling of the subjects and able maintenance of their interests; sixth, dauntless courage in defense of the homeland and repulsion of its enemies; and seventh, notable Qurayshite [55] descent.

Disqualification: There are two important factors that may disqualify a supreme leader from his office: lack of justice [56] and physical disability [57]. The latter is divided into three kinds: missing senses (i.e. loss of reason [58], sight [59], hearing, speech or loss senses that do not affect the office of the sovereign such as smell), missing organs [60], and mental deficiency.

Responsibility: Once the supreme leader has been identified and started managing his administration. He is required to establish his deputies [61] to whom he delegates authority. These are the ministers, governors, appointees who have particular jurisdiction but over unlimited territory (e.g., chief judge, command-in-chief, defender of the borders, and collector of the land tax and legal alms), and appointees who have special jurisdiction in a particular territory (e.g., local judge, land-tax agent, legal-alms collector, defender of the frontier, and garrison commander in a certain district). Ten necessary public duties [62] were laid down by al-Mawardi:

1. He must guard the faith, upholding its established sources and the consensus of the nation's ancestors, arguing with emerging heretics or suspicious dissenters, demonstrating the truth to them and administering to them the legal penalties, so that the faith should remain pristine and the nation free from error.

2. He must enforce law between disputing parties and end disagreement among antagonists until justice prevails and there are no more oppressors or oppressed people.

3. He must protect the country and the household, so that all may go about the business of living and travel anywhere unworried by deception or loss of life or property.

4. He must dispense the legal punishments so that God's prohibitions are observed and His worshippers' rights may be protected from vandalism or misappropriation.

5. He must strengthen border posts by deterrent equipment and fighting force so that the enemies may not gain the

chance to violate what is sanctified or shed a Muslim's or protected non-Muslim's blood.

6. He must fight those who resist the supremacy of Islam after being invited to embrace it, until they convert or sign a treaty of subjection, so that God's claim to have the faith superior to any other is established.

7. He must collect taxes and alms imposed by jurisprudence, on the basis of explicit text and the exercise of judgment, intrepidly but without tyranny.

8. He has to estimate the payments and allocations that must be made by the treasury without extravagance or niggardliness, and pay them neither before nor after the appointed time.

9. He must appoint men who are reliable and sincere and of good counsel to perform the functions or take care of the funds he charges them with in order to ensure efficiency and honest management.

10. He has to oversee matters personally and study the conditions of the people in order to manage public policy and guard the faith instead of relying on delegation of authority

while he is preoccupied with pleasure or worship, for those deemed honest do sometimes betray the trust, and counselors may deceive.

The King of Nizam al-Mulk: Hasan ibn 'Ali of Tus or popularly known with his noble title as Nizam al-Mulk, the chief minister of the administration of the great empire of the Saljuq, had first served Sultan Alp Arslan and then his son Malikshah for over 30 years. Coincidentally, the rise and fall of the Saljuqs coincided with Nizam al-Mulk's birth and demise. According to two sources, he was born either in 408 AH/1018 AD (*Mujmal-I Fasihi*) or in 410 AH/1020 AD (*Tarikh-I Baihaq*); and died in 485/1092, murdered by one of the assassins of the Isma'ilis whom he denounced so fiercely in his book, *Siyasatnama.* [63] He is also a staunch supporter of promoting orthodox religious education, where he founded madrasas or colleges of higher learning in several cities. They were known as Nizamiyyas after him, and the most famous of them were at Baghdad and Nishapur. [64]

Sultan Malikshah commissioned all his political advisers (vazirs) to produce treatises on the art of government because he was so dissatisfied with the current state of his empire. [65] The selection of Nizam al-Mulk's treatise (i.e. the Siyasatnama) over other treatises as the sole handbook of protocols for governance was never known. [66]

In his treatise [67] (the title is written above), he drew up a set of governmental protocols and different aspects of governing the empire, specifically written for Malikshah's regime. Nizam told stories from a historical perspective to show that a weak regime can be cured when a just king refrain from collaborating with evil-doers. According to him, a king must have right judgment, an effective vizier, and officers of virtue. Every task must have proper and suitable worker. While heretics are put down and the orthodox are raised up. Tyrants are repressed, soldiers as well as peasants fear the king, the uneducated is not given position, the inexperienced are not promoted, advice is sought from the intelligent and mature, and men are selected for their skill and not because of their money. In addition, it raises the point that religion is not sold for worldly things, everything is ordered according to merit, thus all people have work according to their capability, and all things are regulated by justice and government by the grace of God. [68]

Selection: It is quite vague to understand how a king must be chosen. According to Nizam al-Mulk, that "in every age and time God (be He exalted) chooses one member of the human race and. having endowed him with goodly and kingly virtues, entrusts him with the interests of the world and the well-being of His servants." [69] Then, it is stated that by divine decree the king "acquires some prosperity and power, and truth bestows good fortune upon him and gives him wit and wisdom, by which he may employ his subordinates according to his merits and confer upon each a dignity and a station proportionate to his powers". [70]

Qualification: For a man to become a full-pledged king, he must have these innate qualities. It is necessary that the king must have "a comely appearance, a kindly disposition, integrity, manliness, bravery, horsemanship, knowledge, (skill in) the use of various kinds of arms, accomplishment in several arts, pity and mercy upon the creatures of God, (strictness in) the performance of vows and promises, sound faith and true belief, devotion to the worship of God and the practice of such virtuous deeds as praying in the nights [71], supererogatory fasting, respect for religious authorities, honoring devout and pious men, patronizing men of learning and wisdom, giving regular alms, doing good to the poor, being kind to subordinates and servants, and relieving the people of oppressors." [72]

Responsibility: It is in Nizam al-Mulk's understanding that God "charges a king to close the doors of corruption, confusion and discord, and He imparts to him such dignity and majesty in the eyes and hearts of men, that under his just rule they may live their lives in constant security and ever wish for his reign to continue." [73]

The king has the duty to "select his ministers and their functionaries from among the people, and giving a rank and post to each, he relies upon them for the efficient conduct of affairs spiritual and temporal. If his subjects tread the path of obedience and busy themselves with their tasks he will keep them untroubled by hardships, so that they may duly pass their time in the shadow of his justice. If one of his officers or ministers commits any impropriety or oppression, he will only keep him at his post provided that he responds to correction, advice or punishment, and wakes up from the sleep of negligence. However, if he fails to mend his ways, he will retain him no longer, but change him for someone who deserves the post. When his subjects are ungrateful for benefits and do not appreciate security and ease, but ponder treachery in their hearts, showing unruliness and overstepping their bounds, he will admonish them for their misdeeds, and punish them in proportion to their crimes." [74]

Function: Aside from the general responsibilities of the King, he also has specific functions in the creation of super infrastructures (in al-Mulk's words, 'advancing the civilization'). The king must "construct underground channels, dig main canals, build bridges across great waters, rehabilitate villages and farms, raise fortifications, build new towns, erect lofty buildings and magnificent dwellings, build inns for travelers along the highways, and schools for those who seek knowledge." [75]

It is also one of the functions of the king to always practice justice and virtue but with specificities as stated by al-Mulk. He said that "it is absolutely necessary that on two days in the week the king should sit for the redress of wrongs, to extract recompense from the oppressor, to give justice and to listen to the words of his subjects with his own ears, without any intermediary. It is fitting that some written petitions should also be submitted if they are comparatively important, and he should give a ruling on each one." [76] In addition, the king should not be hasty in decision and that there must be a thorough investigation and research before making a conclusion or judgment. He argued that "for hastiness is a mark of weakness, not a sign of strength." [77]

A king must always take into account, particularly in urgent matters or business, to consult his counsel with wise elders, loyal supporters, and ministers of state. For al-Mulk "a man who does not take counsel in affairs shows weak judgment ... No task can be accomplished without men of the proper skill; no more can any enterprise succeed without deliberation." [78]

Evaluation: Firstly, it is important to note that the servants (for al-Mulk) have accorded rights to record "those good qualities that are indispensible to a king, and make note of every principle which kings have followed in the past but now do not observe, indicating what is good and what is bad, whatever came to the mind of his humble servant that he had seen, learnt, read or heard...." [79] And, secondly, it is certain that God will judge the king for "on that great day he will be asked to answer for all those of God's creatures who are under his command, and if he tries to transfer (his responsibility) to someone else he will not be listened to. Since this is so, it behooves the king not to leave this important matter to anyone else, and not to disregard the state of God's creatures." [80]

Punishment: Nizam al-Mulk emphasizes the wrath of The Truth (God) if "there occurs any disobedience or disregard of divine laws on the part of His servants, or any failure in devotion and attention to the commands of The Truth (be He exalted), and He wishes to chasten them and make them taste the retribution for their deeds ... verily the wrath of The Truth overtakes those people and He forsakes them for the vileness of their disobedience." [81] In addition, it is God alone according to al-Mulk that "kingship disappears altogether, opposing swords are drawn, blood is shed, and whoever has the stronger hand does whatever he wishes, until those sinners are all destroyed in tumults and bloodshed, and the world becomes free and clear of them; and through the wickedness of such sinners many innocent persons too perish in the tumults." [82] It is quite interesting that these warnings were written in the beginning of chapter I (On the turn of Fortune's wheel and in praise of The Master of the World – may Allah confirm his Sovereignty).

Boon-Companions: According to Nizam al-Mulk, "a king cannot do without suitable boon-companions with whom he can enjoy complete freedom and intimacy." [83] As a general rule, boon-companions [84] cannot be government officials and vice versa because they may "indulge in high-handed practices and oppress the people." For al-Mulk, there are advantages for the necessity of boon-companions because: "firstly, they are company for the king; secondly, since they are with him day and night, they are in the position of bodyguards, and if any danger should appear, they will not hesitate to shield the king from it with their own bodies; thirdly, the king can say thousand different things, serious and frivolous, to his boon-companions which would not be suitable for the ears of his vazir or other nobles; and lastly, all sorts of sundry tidings can be heard from boon-companions, for through their freedom they can report on matters, good and bad, whether drunk or sober...." [85]

Thus, it leads Nizam al-Mulk to conclude that to know the character of the king you have to see if his boon-companions are good or bad.

Comparison of their Views on the Agent (Virtuous Ruler, Shah, Supreme Leader, and King) of Statecrafting a Civilization: Their classical works provided guidelines for all nations in choosing and knowing the qualities, responsibilities, functions, and other pertinent information regarding the essence of becoming a leader and of leadership as well. But, to whom has more efficacies in terms of their views to leadership comparable with the head of state (president or prime minister) in today's world?

On Selection: Al-Farabi's view is more on the result or output of a community that naturally convene themselves because it is necessary for each partaking members. His political organization is an 'association of peoples' who are in symbiotic with one another. And, the most refined among the members (in terms of philosophical knowledge and potential persuasion to convince people with his line of thinking and position in addressing certain significant issues) must be automatically qualified for the position of becoming the virtuous leader. However, the question that someone may ask is 'what are the specific technical procedures and protocols in selecting the virtuous ruler?' This also includes inquiry on testing tools to examine and verify his character as a virtuous individual.

Ferdowsi's view is significantly related with political institutions of monarchy, totalitarian type of leadership, and dynasty of familial regimes. An individual can only become shah if he is appointed or selected by the out-going shah or if it is hereditary (i.e. originated from previous generations of royal family-based rulers). Unfortunately, these types of political regimes do exist today. You can find them from East Asia, Africa, to South America, etc., although, some monarchies hold titular (symbolical) representations only. Nepotism, cronyism, and favoritism are often the causes of these regimes that usually lead them to their downfall (i.e. if the welfare of his people is not seriously taken care of or dealt with).

Nizam al-Mulk's view is vague regarding the process of selecting a leader. He contends for a divine intervention and only in this manner that a leader can be determined. I contend that since he is writing for a specific person, the Sultan of the Saljuq Empire, he is providing valuable prominence in defining the status of the leader. In short, he wanted to please and show that the Sultan is divinely chosen as the sole steward of God's creation thus giving him a pedestal of automatic power and wide proximal influence all over his territories. In addition, the leader has innate characteristics of goodly and kingly virtues and receiver of wealth, power, wit, and wisdom for he was the righteous one determined by God through his message given to the Prophet.

While al-Mawardi is more technical and jurisprudential that is backed up by historical traditions and recorded (documented) reports to show evidences supporting his ideas and claims. His ideas of having electors suggest a representative democracy but in the veins of oligarchy because you have few chosen people who have the sole authority in selecting the supreme leader. Although, he provided us about how a person can be a member of electors; it remains unclear on who or how a person can become an elector. Elector's criteria of probity, knowledge, wisdom, and prudence are difficult to find to a man because they need more years of trainings and development of their expertise. You also need to survey societies by asking each of the inhabitants who have gained their high respect and admiration congruent with the characters mentioned above, thus it may lead you to identify and nominate the members for the electors. The numbers of electors are also contested as shown with different opinions from jurists. It may even be reduced to one, i.e., appointed by the incumbent official.

Ferdowsi and Nizam al-Mulk have similarities in terms of selecting the leader (agent of statecraft) and that is through the prerogative of the incumbent leader or if it is divinely intervened. And, al-Farabi's 'societies of peoples' and al-Mawardi's 'body of electors' have democratic inclinations (where, at least, the leader is selected by his community itself or the people have a role in choosing their representative).

On Qualification: All four of them agreed that a leader must be intelligent, and has the wisdom and knowledge of public administration and governance, but al-Farabi takes it to a different (higher) level categorizing the leader as a philosopher (which meant that he innately acquired all the intellectual faculties of a philosopher as distinctly listed in his 12 qualities and 6 conditions to become a virtuous ruler). Moreover, al-Farabi added the power of imagination and charisma (power of persuasion) as a salient quality of a leader.

On the other hand, Ferdowsi gave importance of the virtue of courage and bravery as significant assets of a leader. Another similarity is that they did not specify whether a woman can be a leader, but hinted on masculine qualities, characteristics and/or roles typical to a man.

Both al-Mawardi and Nizam al-Mulk believed that a leader must be morally pious and believer of Islam, physically fit for the position in order to become effective in handling his tasks and duties, and has the audacity and courage to provide security for his subjects and territories. However, al-Mawardi included that he must be a descendant of the Quraysh community as supported by Islamic traditions and documented reports. While al-Mulk gives precedental importance to the aesthetic outlook of the leader having a comely appearance, a kindly disposition, manliness, and knows the art of horsemanship since Saljuqs are well-known horsemen.

In short, a leader must be knowledgeable, faithful, brave, risk-taker, and physically fit for the position. However, none of them argued that a leader is someone that knows how to listen to his constituencies and manifests the virtue of humility.

On Responsibility: All argued for specific duties and tasks for the leader with the obligation to immediately create and organize his administration by appointing particular persons appropriate for the job, but no one argued for establishing a consultative body in order to review, evaluate, and confirm his nominated individuals for their specific post. Thus, the leader has the utmost authority, leniency, and prerogative as to whom he would give the position, which usually leads to problematic favoritism, cronyism, and nepotism. And, basically roots of dictatorship will soon start to spread all over his dominion. In addition, since he has the power to appoint, he also has the power to remove or persecute them as long as those individuals are guilty of their crimes. In this regard, the leader must be just, virtuous, and morally apt in order to conclude a verdict to the suspect.

According to the recurring stories in Shahnameh, Ferdowsi's primary duty for the leader is to protect his dominion from insecurities such as poverty, famine, threats from external forces (impending invasions), and maintain stability, peace and order all over his territorial jurisdiction. This is probably the main reason why he gave importance to courage as a major quality of the leader. For al-Farabi, in order for the leader to instruct the elite and form their character, he ought to be a philosopher skilled in the speculative sciences, and in order for him to instruct the masses and form their character, he ought to be a prophet who possesses persuasion and imagination to perfection. In short, a combination of two professions: philosopher and prophet.

Al-Mawardi highlighted that his leader must uphold faith, protect the people by destroying forces threatening the foundation of their Islamic faith, and fight those who resist the supremacy of Islam, while al-Mulk pays concrete attention to expanding and building more infrastructures for the Saljuq Empire. In this regard, al-Mawardi argues for theoretically strengthening the Islamic faith, while al-Mulk argues for materialistic wealth and power in order to bring peace and order in the whole Muslim empire.

If you will pay more attention, you may correlate their views of the tasks and responsibilities of their leader in today's actual professions, i.e., academic professor (for al-Farabi), military general (for Ferdowsi), pope (for al-Mawardi), and industrial engineer (for Nizam al-Mulk).

On Other Observations: Al-Farabi likened his virtuous state into a modern bureaucratic government where each official have specific roles and duties but in a hierarchical (pyramid) system. That is, there is a top level position with its own subordinates, while those subordinates have also their own (lower) subordinates. Their primal responsibility is to maintain an organized institution where the top rank official is satisfactorily served by his subordinates, and these subordinates are also satisfactorily served by their own subordinates. Protocols of their duties are respectfully followed, maintained, and preserved. He also elaborated on his ideas of imperfect states: ignorant, ruined, declined, and lost/misled states. You can find some related variables of his imperfect states comparable with democracy, capitalism, socialism, and communism.

Both Ferdowsi and Nizam al-Mulk have emphasized the wrath of God in reprimanding leaders who are disobedient of His rules. Al-Mawardi did not provide details about punishment of the leader but he provided a section on disqualification from becoming the sovereign Imam, which he centered on committed injustices (acts) and detailed conditions and factors relating to physical disability. Thus, al-Mawardi is traditionalist in upholding and maintaining the traditions documented through the sources (Qur'an, Hadith, and consensual decisions and respected arguments from other jurists, theologians, and commentators alike) of Islam.

Nizam al-Mulk is somehow innovative in terms of providing evaluative process to assess the current track record of the leader, even though he is particularly addressing his Sultan's demands, wants, and needs in order to satisfy and please him. Thus, he provided a full chapter on boon-companion and literally emphasizing that his leader is the entrusted steward by God and of His creation.

It is no wonder that al-Mawardi's work is highly regarded and recognized as a major reference discussed and quoted in courses on Islamic political thought, law, and government. For many scholars, it has been described as the standard formulation of the orthodox Sunni's Islamic theory of government, but for others contend that there is no such thing as a single received Sunni theory of government because they view the book as an attempt by al-Mawardi to reconcile a certain interpretation of Islamic law, the Ash'arite doctrine (one of several existing or possible theoretical positions on the subject) with the political realities under the Buyids.[86

The *Siyasatnama* became a classic on its own paving the way to reorganize the administrative system of the Saljuq Empire and inspiring the establishment of the Ottoman Empire, one of the longest polities existed in the world. Thus, the impacts and influences of these selected works can still be felt in the contemporary world, from monarchical parliamentary form of government to presidential one, and referenced as blueprint for the creation of standard operating procedures and protocols for a bureaucratic system of a modern world.

REFERENCES

1. There is a thin demarcation of meanings between a state and a nation. And that is the degree of homogeneity of society of peoples coming from their affinities with belief system (political ideology), religion, language, traditions, and culture. However, both state and nation have definite territories (composed of land, water, and air/space which are determined by boundaries), population (citizenship/nationality), government (leadership style), and sovereignty (supreme or final authority of a political entity over its own affairs and is

recognized externally). Thus, nation-state is commonly used today and attributed to the Treaty of Westphalia in 1648. It is also important to note the emerging literature on civilization-state as opposed to merely nation-state. The United States, Europe, China, India, and the Islamicate civilization are examples of civilization-state. For further information, see Peter J. Katzenstein. *Civilizations in World Politics: Plural and Pluralist Perspectives*. London, UK: Routledge, 2009.

2.   His most important analysis is his section on the 'Axial Transition'. For example, in ancient Greek civilization he pointed out four factors, including 1) emergence of polis and importance of the cult of Olympian deities as the focus of solidarity in developing polis, i.e. political development; 2) literacy development, i.e. development of arts and humanities; 3) invention of money, i.e. economic development; and 4) increasing rationalization of Greek thought, i.e. development of architectural technology as suggested by Robert Hahn. Although, he argued that Plato and Socrates signify the completion of axial transition in ancient Greece. In conclusion, he said that the death of Socrates and end of political independence of Athenians did not hamper the dissemination of ideas and knowledge, but resulted to a spillover of disciples of different schools of thoughts, philosophies, and progressed to other polis and/or societies, e.g., Platonic Academy, Aristotle's Lyceum, Stoics, Epicureans, imitations by the Macedonians and Romans (although restrictions and

intolerance occurred with the dominance of the Christian Church), etc. In short, the failure of the Greek polis did not mean the failure of the Greek culture which is the schools per se, e.g. gymnasia, philosophy, medicine, and arts. For more details regarding axial transitions of civilizations, see Robert N. Bellah. *Religion in Human Evolution: From the Paleolethic to the Axial Age*. Cambridge et al: Harvard University Press, 2011.

3. An encyclopedic entry written by Eisenstadt for the 2001 International Encyclopedia of the Social and Behavioral Sciences, and it is accessible at <http://www.sciencedirect.com/science/article/pii/B008043076 7008226>.

4. Marshall G.S. Hodgson. The Venture of Islam: Conscience and History in a World Civilization (Vol. I: The Classical Age of Islam). Chicago, USA: University Of Chicago Press, 1977, p. 91.

5. Ibn Khaldun. *The Muqaddimah: An Introduction to History*. Translated by Franz Rosenthal and with Introduction by Bruce Lawrence, (Abridged Edition), New Jersey, USA: Princeton University Press, 2004.

6. Hodgson emphasized the keen consciousness of the world Muslim community. He further explains that "they are moved by a sense of universal Muslim solidarity, and maintain in the most diverse geography not only the essential distinctive Islamic rites - including the great common pilgrimage to

Mecca where all nations may meet - but also, to some degree, a sense of a common cultural heritage." Thus, Islam is the common denominator between Hodgson and Ibn Khaldun, as they see it as the core element in studying the pluralistic identities and mapping out the historiographies of Muslim communities - be they in different sections or categories such as individuality, ethnicity, society, linguality, geography, demography, ancestry, etc. Another singular denominator between Hodgson and Ibn Khaldun is the notion on allegiance. For Ibn Khaldun, strong allegiance originates from (blood) relationship and common lineage and descent. On the other hand, Hodgson sees strong allegiance via confessional religiosity and its traditions is somewhat populistic because "they tended to cast their doctrines and their moral standards into forms intelligible to the ordinary person."

7. Norbert Elias. *The Civilizing Process: State Formation and Civilization (Vol. II)*, Oxford: Blackwell, 1982.

8. There were inconsistencies regarding his full name and date of birth: some Arabic sources say his complete name is *Muhammad Ibn Muhammad Ibn Uzalagh Ibn Tarkhan* and others state *Abū Naṣr Muḥammad ibn Muḥammad Fārābī* or *Abu Nasr ibn Muhammad ibn Muhammad ibn Tarkhan ibn Uzlag Al-Farabi*. In the West he is known as *Alpharabius*. He is said to have been a native of Farab in Transoxiana and of Turkish or Turkoman origin. He was born in 870 or 872 in the district of the city of Farab in Turkestan or in Otrar (located in

present-day Kazakhstan). Following his visit to Egypt in 949, he returned to Damascus (located in present-day Syria), where he died in 950.

9. See: Fakhry, Majid. *Al-Farabi, Founder of Islamic Neoplatonism: His Life, Works, and Influence.* Oxford, UK: Oneworld Publications, 2002, pp. 1-6.

10. Ibid. pp. 211-214.

11. See: Hammond, Robert. *The Philosophy of Alfarabi.* New York: The Hobson Book Press, 1947.

12. Fakhry, Majid. *Al-Farabi, Founder of Islamic Neoplatonism: His Life, Works, and Influence.* Oxford, UK: Oneworld Publications, 2002, p. 101.

13. See: Al-Farabi. *The Perfect State: Mabadi' ara' ahl al-Madina al-Faḍila: A Revised Text with Introduction, Translation, and Commentary.* Trans. Richard Walzer. Gloucestershire, UK: Clarendon Press, 1985.

14. Al-Farabi, p. 42.

15. Ibid. p. 75.

16. Ibid. p. 79.

17. Ibid. p. 48.

18. Sjadzali, Munawir. *Islam and Governmental System.* Jakarta: Indonesian-Netherlands Cooperation in Islamic Studies (INIS), 1991, p. 36.

19. Farhat-Holzman, Laina. "The Shahnameh of Ferdowsi: An Icon to National Identity," *Comparative Civilizations Review*, No. 44, Spring 2001, p. 104.

20. The Shahaname is a collection of pre-Islamic stories, legends, history, myths and poems that had been told by storytellers, grandparents and holy men for hundreds and hundreds of years. It was collected and written by Hakim Abul-Qasim Firdawsi Tusi or simply Ferdowsi.

21. Ibid, p. 105.

22. See Ferdowsi and the Shahnameh accessible at <http://shahnameh.eu/ferdowsi.html>.

23. See Clayton, Sally Pomme. "Shahname Synopsis," British Library: Learning Inside History (2005). Accessed at <http://www.bl.uk/learning/cult/inside/corner/shah/synopsis.html>.

24. Further details at Shahnameh at pages 3-4.

25. He is not related (by blood) with Kaiumers.

26. The son of Ahriman, the evil, who is very jealous with Kaiumers' status throughout the cosmos of the universe.

27. Son of Tahumers. Tahumers ruled the world for 30 years and died naturally.

28. Shahnameh, p. 6.

29. Ibid, p. 5.

30. The 7 heroic trials were summarized at <http://www.bl.uk/learning/cult/inside/corner/shah/synopsis.html>. You can also find some similarities with the trials of Hercules in Rustem's stories.

31. He is the sone of Zal and Rudabeh who reigned for 300 years.

32. Rustem's war horse.

33. Rakush saved Rustem life while he's asleep.

34. Rustem and Rakush test of religious faith is displayed.

35. Whenever Rakush would wake Rustem, he immediately gets irritated and reprimand Rakush which happened twice.

36. After all the trials and adventures, Rustem fulfilled his mission to set Kavus free from captivity from the demons.

37. The Shahs of Old, pp. 6-7.

38. See footnote no. 11.

39. Ibid, p. 6.

40. Ibid, pp. 6-7.

41. See footnote no. 23.

42. Ibid of footnote no. 23.

43. Dates of his birth and demise were taken from the Translator's Introduction at page xii of al-Mawardi's *The Ordinances of Government*.

44. Ibid, p. xiii.

45. *"Al-Ahkam Al-Sultaniyyah: The Laws of Islamic Governance* by Asadullah Yate; and *The Ordinances of Government: A Translation of Al-Ahkam Al-Sultaniyya A'Al-Wilayat Al-Diniyya* by Wafaa H. Wahba."* Review by: Ingrid Mattson, *Journal of Law and Religion*. Vol. 15, No. 1/2 (2000 - 2001), pp. 399-403. Stable URL: http://www.jstor.org/stable/ 1051533

46. Third section of the first chapter located at page 5.

47. It's the first section of the first chapter (On the appointment of the Sovereign {Imam}) located at page 4.

48. Third section of the same chapter located at page 5.

49. Fourth section of the first chapter located at page 6.

50. Fifth section, p. 8-9.

51. Al-Mawardi argued that, in p. 9, "should an incumbent, therefore wish to nominate a successor, he must do his best to find the one most qualified for it ... he must first ascertain whether he is a son or a father; if not, he may appoint him to office without participation from anyone else, and even without consulting the electors." All that the supreme leader needs is the acceptance from the one he nominated to take his appointment into effect. However, if on the other hand, the successor is a son or a father there are three acceptable approaches in pp. 9-10: first, he may not nominate a son or father until he consults the electors and they judge his nominee suitable for the office; second, accords him the right to decide independently whether to nominate a son or father, because he is the sovereign, whose word is command for the nation to obey whether believed to be in its interest or against it; and third, he has the authority to appoint his father but not his son, as one is by nature more partial to one's son than to one's father, and is therefore inclined to amass wealth mostly for the benefit of the child rather than the parent.

52. Ibid, p. 7.

53. Now, this is where al-Mawardi contrived the legitimacy of dictatorship for he allows that the selection of a leader can be reduced to singular entity. In addition, in page 7, he opined that there should only be one sovereign ruler.

54. Ibid, p. 4. It's the second section of the same chapter.

55. This condition, according to al-Mawardi, is a matter indisputably settled by explicit text and by general consensus. For it was from the own words of the Prophet that "Imams (leaders) come from Quraysh."

56. It pertains to sinfulness, committing forbidden deeds and venturing on violations of decency in pursuit of pleasure. See page 17 of the 11th section of the first chapter.

57. This has something to do with suspected unorthodoxy, which would preempt investiture and continuation in office in the opinion of some scholars, on the ground that mere suspicion is sufficient as in the case of utter disbelief. See page 17 of the 11th section of the first chapter.

58. Refers to chronic diseases such as madness or idiocy.

59. With the exemption of night-blindness and poor vision, for they can still continue their office.

60. This has four categories: First, those that do not affect the validity of appointment or continued tenure in office (e.g., removal of penis or testicles); second, those that preclude appointment to the office of the Caliph and continued tenure in it (e.g., loss of the hands or legs invalidate himself from becoming the supreme leader); third, those that preclude appointment to office but there is disagreement on its effect on continued tenure (e.g., partial disablement from work due to loss of one arm or leg which excludes the candidate for appointment); and fourth, those that do not prevent an

incumbent from remaining in office but there is disagreement on the question of the legitimacy of conferring te office on a candidate suffering from it (e.g., disfigurement of face or ugliness, mutilated nose or gouged eye). Further details are elaborated in pp. 19-20.

61. Ibid, pp. 21-22. 14th section of the first chapter.

62. 10th section of the first chapter at page 16. Duties are copied verbatim to emphasize specific obligations and activities provided by the author.

63. The dates of his birth and death were taken from the same book (Siyasatnama) located in the introduction part at page ix.

64. Ibid, p. x. In Nishapur, he recruited al-Ghazali to become a professor and later invited him to join in his court as one of the highly respected viziers.

65. Ibid, p. xi. The current state of his empire pertains to the disorganized system of his administration. So Malikshah started a project to have the best blueprint of government protocols and bureaucratic (or standard) procedures to centralized the whole empire.

66. It was not documented how his treatise was selected by Sultan Malikshah, but my hunch is that he did his own way by playing some dirty tricks just like what he did to al-Kanduri, another vazir (minister), clandestinely ordered to be executed. Nizam al-Mulk perceived al-Knaduri as an obstacle or threat for his ambition to become the 'khwaja (master) of the world' under the empire of Saljuq.

67. Where all quotations and citations will be referred continuously in this essay.

68. M. A. Zaidi's review published on13 May 2002 at <http://www.amazon.com/The-Book-Government-Rules-Kings/dp/0700712283>.

69. Most of his arguments regarding the king can be found in chapter 1 (On the turn of Fortune's wheel and in praise of The Master of the World – may Allah confirm his Sovereignty) located in pp. 9-11.

70. Ibid, p. 9.

71. He added that in addition to the five prescribed times of prayer, the king must devote his evening times to God.

72. Ibid, pp. 10-11. You may notice that following the principles of Islam is an integral part of becoming a king for Nizam al-Mulk.

73. Similar page, but he did not elaborate on the technicalities of the operation on how God give orders to the king, instead my personal hunch is that the instructions and orders of God can be found in the sources (Qur'an and Hadith) of Islam.

74. A long quotation located in page 10. The subsequent sentences refer to the specific functions of the King.

75. As stated in footnote no. 11. It is explicitly manifested that Nizam al-Mulk is obsessed with the aesthetics of the empire that needs to specifically list them for Malikshah's pleasure.

76. "Chapter III: On holding court for the redress of wrongs and practicing justice and virtue" located at page 13.

77. "Chapter XXXVIII: On the inadvisability of hastiness in affairs on the part of kings" located at page 129.

78. "Chapter XVIII: On having consultation with learned and experience men" located at page 92.

79. Ibid, p. 11. It is interesting to note that al-Mulk divided the evaluation process of a king's track record into human (material) and God (divine) assessments.

80. "Chapter II: On recognizing the extent of God's grace towards kings" located at page 13.

81. This quotation can be found in page 9 of the first chapter after al-Mulk wrote that God is the sole authority in choosing the king, while God also has the power to remove him.

82. Ibid, p. 9.

83. "Chapter XVII: Concerning boon-companions and intimates of the king and the conduct of affairs" located at pp.89-91.

84. There are several criteria for a suitable boon-companion. Nizam al-Mulk argued that "he must be well bred, accomplished and of cheerful face. He should have pure faith, be able to keep secrets and wear good clothes. He must possess an ample fund of stories and strange tales both amusing and serious, and be able to tell them well. He must always be good talker and a pleasant partner; he should know how to play backgammon and chess, and if he can play a harp and other musical instruments, so much the better. He must always agree with the king.... Where pleasure and entertainment are concerned, as in feasting, drinking, hunting, polo and gaming –

in all matters like these it is right that the king should consult with his boon-companions...."

85. Ibid, p. 89.

86. Further contentions and arguments on al-Mawardi's book are presented in the Translator's Introduction of the same book located at page xiv.